Ministry of Defence

The Government's Response to the

Deepcut Review

Presented to Parliament by
The Secretary of State for Defence
By Command of Her Majesty

June 2006

© Crown Copyright 2006

Cm 6851

£6.15

The Establishment of the Deepcut Review

1. On 30 November 2004, the Minister of State for the Armed Forces, the Rt Hon Adam Ingram MP, announced to the House of Commons that he proposed to commission a review. The terms of reference were:

   "Urgently to review the circumstances surrounding the deaths of four soldiers at Princess Royal Barracks, Deepcut, between 1995 and 2002 in light of available material and any representations that might be made in this regard, and to produce a report."

   Nicholas Blake QC agreed to undertake the review.

2. The four soldiers were Private Sean Benton (died 9 June 1995), Private Cheryl James (died 27 November 1995), Private Geoff Gray (died 17 September 2001) and Private James Collinson (died 23 March 2002). All were Royal Logistic Corps soldiers undergoing training at Deepcut Barracks. All had died from gunshot wounds while performing guard duty. The investigations into their deaths involved the Royal Military Police, the Surrey Police and HM Coroner for Surrey, who conducted the inquests.

3. The death of James Collinson led to Surrey Police re-opening the investigations into the three earlier deaths. By September 2003 the investigations into each of the deaths had been completed and four reports, one for each death, were written, summarising the conclusions and outcome. During their investigations, Surrey Police had seen 900 witnesses, taken over 1,500 evidential statements and commissioned independent forensic and ballistic examinations. No evidence of third party involvement in any of the deaths had been uncovered. The reports were provided to the Coroner on 19 September 2003. The report into the death of James Collinson would assist the Coroner into the inquest he was to hold into that death; inquests had already been held into the earlier deaths. On 13 October 2003 the Coroner wrote to the legal representatives of the families notifying them that, in his opinion, the reports did not reveal sufficient new information to suggest that different verdicts would necessarily result if fresh inquests were held.

4. Concerns about the care and supervision of trainee soldiers, which had arisen in the course of their investigations, led the Surrey Police to initiate discussions with the Army, which led in August 2002 to the creation of a joint 'Learning Account' to review risk factors and identify the lessons to be learned. It also led the Surrey Police to publish their Fifth Report ('Deepcut Investigation Final Report') in March 2004. This report called for a broader enquiry into issues it had raised concerning the training of young soldiers and the disciplinary environment in which they found themselves. In that month, the House of Commons Defence Select Committee launched a major inquiry of its own looking into the duty of care regimes in initial training establishments of all three Armed Forces. Their report was published in March 2005, while Nicholas Blake's review was in progress.

5. The Deepcut Review was published on 29 March 2006, having been delayed so that it could take into account the final inquest, into the death of James Collinson, which began to hear evidence on 20 February 2006.

The Government's Response to the Deepcut Review

6. This paper sets out the Government's response to the Deepcut Review. Each of the four deaths was a tragedy in its own right and we extend our sincere condolences to those families who mourn loved ones lost to untimely deaths.

7. The Government welcomes the Review, undertaken by Nicholas Blake QC, which we are confident represents an independent, objective and comprehensive analysis of all matters which have a bearing on the four deaths. We acknowledge that mistakes were made and that there were deficiencies in the systems of care for young and sometimes vulnerable trainees. We take our responsibility to ensure the wellbeing and safety of all our personnel extremely seriously and we are committed to continuous improvement in this respect. Much progress has already been made, but the recommendations of the Deepcut Review will add momentum to our programme of change.

8. The Deepcut Review has concluded that, although the Army did not cause the deaths of the four young soldiers, there were failures to identify potential sources of risk and to address them. Important questions have been raised about the nature of the training environment at the time. The Review also concluded that no new reliable evidence as to how the four soldiers met their deaths is likely to be available, and that on this basis a Public Inquiry is not necessary. We share this view and, given the extensive investigations that have taken place, see no public or Service interest in pursuing a Public Inquiry. We must now ensure that lessons are learned from these tragic events and that we do everything we can to ensure that such incidents do not happen again.

9. The Government accepts the great majority of the recommendations made by the Review, though in a few cases this is with some qualification or modification. In particular, we accept the Review's objective to provide independent assurance that the procedures are working as effectively as they can and that systemic issues of concern are addressed. We propose independent, external inspection and review of the military justice system and the military complaints system, together with independent members on Service complaints panels dealing with complaints of bullying and harassment. We will appoint an independent person as a commissioner to report annually on the fairness and effectiveness of the military complaints system and we will publish his report. He will have direct access to Ministers. That commissioner will also have a power to refer complaints or allegations of bullying or harassment to the Commanding Officer for action; and to be notified of the outcome.

10. Where we have not fully accepted recommendations, we are confident that we can give meaning to the intent behind the recommendation, with the following qualifications: Recommendation 30 (relating to the availability of inquests where death occurs overseas) is a matter that will be decided in relation to the Coroners Bill; Recommendation 31 (availability of legal representation for families at inquests) is not readily reconciled with the general character of inquests; Recommendation 33 is a matter for the Surrey Police.

11. We will use the Deepcut Review as a blueprint for further action. Action is already in progress on many of the matters raised by the Review and the Government is fully committed to sustaining this momentum, and to allocating investment necessary to deliver real, measurable improvements across the spectrum of duty of care.

Response to Recommendations

The recommendations of the Deepcut Review are listed separately below, followed by the Government's response to each. The intention, unless stated otherwise, is to take forward these recommendations across the three Services.

Recommendation 1

Young people with suitable qualities for a military career should continue to be able to enlist at 16, with a view to fully participating in all aspects of military duties from the age of 18, so long as their training takes place in a suitable environment dedicated to the needs of such young people, and particular care is taken for their welfare.

We welcome the Review's conclusion that the Armed Forces should continue to recruit young people from the age of 16. By recruiting under 18s, the Armed Forces provide valuable and constructive training and employment to many young people, giving them a sense of great achievement and worth, as well as benefiting society as a whole.

We appreciate the importance, as highlighted in the Review, of understanding and addressing the particular vulnerabilities and requirements of those under the age of 18. Commanding Officers take their responsibilities towards all their people extremely seriously, and they are well aware of the particular welfare needs of younger recruits and trainees, even if they are not formally in loco parentis. A guidance note for all Commanding Officers has been produced specifically relating to working with under 18s, and this is being reviewed in the light of the Deepcut Review. A "Care of Trainees" module was introduced to the training programme for instructors and other supervisory staff in 2004, and this has been incorporated in the "Train the Trainer" course for instructors, which has been introduced across the Armed Forces. In addition, a new policy on the provision of supervisory care in Phase 1 and 2 training establishments was introduced in March this year, which requires each unit to produce a Supervisory Care Directive. The Directive is based on the thorough assessment of the risk to trainees which takes account of the particular factors pertaining to the establishment and nature of the training being undertaken.

We have accelerated the projects to improve recruits' accommodation at several training establishments and ongoing improvements to the training environment will continue to be taken forward through the Defence Training Review. Under current assumptions, the Defence Training Review will provide over 4000 new accommodation spaces for Phase 2 trainees by 2012.

More widely, a tri-Service review into the provision of a number of aspects of welfare support has been carried out, with a view to harmonising tri-Service standards where appropriate, adopting best practice, and identifying and correcting any perceived weaknesses in welfare delivery.

We will continue to examine the environment in which recruits are trained in order to maintain ongoing improvement.

Recommendation 2

The training environment for those under 18 should have the following features:

i) Those under 17 should be trained in establishments exclusive to this age group.
ii) ATRA should aim to provide the facilities and the length of training presently provided by the AFC Harrogate to all recruits under 17.
iii) In the meantime, Phase 1 training at ATR Bassingbourn should be extended progressively to 26 weeks.

We fully appreciate that the training environment should take into account the specific requirements of recruits and trainees under the age of 18. For the Army, Harrogate and Bassingbourn already provide training facilities exclusively for recruits under the age of 17. But some under 17s are also trained at other training establishments.

From April this year, Army Phase 1 training was extended from 12 to 14 weeks, the course at Bassingbourn for junior soldiers from 17 to 20 weeks, and the combined Phase 1 and 2 infantry course from 24 to 26 weeks.

The Army is now looking further at options of how best to provide training to all young soldiers, including: progressively adjusting the age at which soldiers are recruited into the Army; adjusting the length and balance of academic and military content of training courses; providing additional training and qualifications; and adapting training establishments to configure them better for the needs of young recruits.

However, as we stated in our response to the House of Commons Defence Committee's report on Duty of Care, published in July 2005, it would be difficult to mandate the separation of under 18s in training across the entirety of the Armed Forces. Such separation would create barriers in training that do not reflect the reality of the Service environment and may be undesirable, as well as counter-productive, to the achievement of some training objectives. It nevertheless remains our intention to ensure that the specific needs of those under 18 are being met.

Recommendation 3

Where young people over 17 but under 18 are trained together with adults in Phase 2 training, special provision should be made for their safety, welfare and development in the design of the training regime and the environment in which it is delivered. The Army should plan to eliminate the need for soldiers to join their units in the field army on completion of Phase 1 and 2 training until they reach the age of 18.

Specific direction is given to all Commanding Officers regarding the care of under 18s, to ensure that the particular vulnerabilities and requirements of these young Service people are identified and addressed. This guidance will be amended and re-issued in the light of the Deepcut Review.

Work is underway to consider how we might ensure that trainees have reached the age of 18 before they are posted to their units. This includes looking at slight adjustments to recruiting ages and to the length of training courses. However, it may be neither feasible nor desirable to do so for all disciplines across the Armed Forces, and the practicability of this recommendation needs to be carefully considered alongside the important requirement to reduce the time that trainees spend waiting for either further training or onward posting.

Recommendation 4

The Army should routinely seek confirmation from others of self-declared medical and social histories, including access to medical or other confidential records. Such data is necessary to make a full assessment of the applicant's suitability and enable training centres to be aware of any particular vulnerability that may need addressing.

Whilst information on a recruit's medical background is currently already sought by the Armed Forces, this may not include sight of the full medical record of an applicant or recruit. Since April 2004, however, the Army has sought to obtain sight of the medical records of recruits and a completed health questionnaire from the recruit's GP on arrival at the Phase 1 training establishment. This information is then scrutinised by occupational clinical staff. Evaluation of this process will be carried out and made available to the other two Services.

Recommendation 5

The Army should encourage maximum involvement in the selection process by the parent, or other responsible adult, of the applicant under 18.

We recognise the vital role parents play in support of their children, both before and after they have joined the Armed Forces. Individuals under the age of 18 may only join the Armed Forces if their application is accompanied by the formal written consent of his or her parent or guardian. Subsequently, Recruiting Officers establish and sustain links with the parent(s) or guardian(s) of those who have applied to join the Armed Forces.

Commanding Officers are required to write to the parents or guardians of recruits under the age of 18 on arrival at their unit, providing details of how the unit can be contacted, setting out the training their son or daughter will undertake, and encouraging them to contact the unit if they have any questions or concerns. The same information is available to the families of those over 18, although the Commanding Officer must obtain the trainee's agreement before it is released to them.

Contact with parents continues through training through parents' days that are held during courses and the final passing out ceremony, to which parents and guardians are invited.

We are now examining how contact with parents could further be improved, for example through such media as training establishment websites and bulletin boards; some establishments already have such systems.

Recommendation 6

A clear and concise information pack should be made available for the parent, or responsible adult, before consent is given to recruitment of a minor, explaining:

(i)   what the commitment to a military career involves;
(ii) where and when training will take place;
(iii) where and how further information can be obtained;
(iv) who to turn to if the young person encounters difficulties and problems;
(v)   how long service will be for; and
(vi) when and how the options to leave the Army can be exercised.

Information packs are already provided to recruits and their parents, and these are being reviewed to ensure that they fulfil this recommendation. Updated versions of this information should be available from the summer of this year.

Recommendation 7

Recruits who joined the Army as minors and who have reached a settled decision that they are unhappy with pursuing a military career before they reach the end of their Phase 2 training, but after their 18th birthday, should be able to discharge as of right.

Current Service policy already makes provision for unhappy Service personnel under the age of 18 to leave the Services. Individuals deemed unsuitable for Service life during their training, which may be as a result of their unhappiness or discontentment with their Service, may also be discharged; these individuals in this respect are dealt with on a case by case basis. Additionally, and importantly, under the suicide vulnerability risk management policy, which was introduced into the Army Training and Recruiting Agency (ATRA) in August 2005, minors deemed to be 'at risk' will be discharged, with reports rendered where appropriate, to the relevant civilian authorities.

Work is underway to examine how further measures could be put in place to accommodate trainees who wish to leave the Armed Forces having joined prior to their 18th birthday. However, the length of training courses and the investment in individuals, particularly in the more technical or specialist areas, varies significantly. The longest initial training course is over four years. The implications of allowing an individual to leave as a right at the end of such training therefore need to be carefully considered. In particular, it is very unlikely that, in practice, a trainee who joined the Armed Forces under the age of 18 would, after extensive counselling and support, be forced to have completed such training against his or her will.

Recommendation 8

ATRA should maintain a regular audit of its training estate:

i)   It must be satisfied that it has provided decent, safe, and appropriate facilities for its personnel where the needs for private life and personal development are catered for as well as their military training.
ii) The physical and psychological environment should combine to inspire and motivate the trainee.
iii) If it does not, ATRA must immediately plan to redress this.

Regular health and safety inspections are carried out across the Defence Estate to ensure that it is safe for all trainees and staff. In addition, the Armed Forces' training infrastructure is subject to regular audit. Estate issues have also been examined in the course of inspections by the Directorate of Operational Capability, which is independent of the chain of command, and by the wholly independent Adult Learning Inspectorate.

The Ministry of Defence recognises the importance of providing accommodation and other facilities that are modern, functional and attractive to the trainees. Projects to improve accommodation at several training establishments have now been accelerated and further improvements are envisaged under the Defence Training Review, which aims to rationalise and improve the training estate, incorporating substantial investment. Our aim is that the training environment should instil discipline and purpose, within a context in which both instructors and trainees feel valued as individuals, and are treated with respect. We agree that this is as much about improving the psychological as the physical environment. Training, in all its aspects, and care of personnel generally, are and will remain priority areas.

Recommendation 9

All reasonable measures should be taken to reduce or eliminate delays in Phase 2 training. Wherever there are delays, the trainees should be informed in a written record of the progress to date and the future timetable.

Every effort is made to ensure that the number of personnel awaiting Phase 2 training is kept to a necessary minimum. Much progress has already been made and the majority of trainees do not have to wait to attend trade training courses. We intend this progress to continue. Those awaiting Phase 2 courses conduct structured military skills training, adventure training and educational programmes. It is inevitable that certain factors, such as illness or a failure to pass a course element, will also cause delays. Where any delays occur, individuals should be fully briefed and are provided with a relevant programme of activities. Alternatively, they may be offered a transfer to another branch or trade. From June this year, the Army Training and Recruitment Agency (ATRA) is introducing new procedures whereby each trainee is given a copy of his or her individual training plan for Phase 2 before they leave Phase 1 training. Should this plan be amended, an updated version will be issued.

Recommendation 10

ATRA should require all its training regiments to identify the supervisory ratios it needs to train future generations of trainees in accordance with the effective duty of care principles outlined in this Report. Those ratios should be taken as the necessary minimum, in the absence of any subsequent comprehensive risk assessment to revise them.

We accept that levels of supervision in the past, particularly at some Phase 2 training establishments, have been too low, as indicated in the Review, and we have endeavoured to address this. Whilst the adding back of 179 military staff posts into the Army Training Organisation has undoubtedly helped to improve the situation, a number of other measures have also been implemented across all three Services to improve the effectiveness of the care of trainees. Arrangements for supervision are reviewed as part of the programmes of inspection carried out by the independent Adult Learning Inspectorate.

A new policy on the provision of supervisory care in Phase 1 and 2 training establishments was introduced in March this year, which requires each unit to produce a Supervisory Care Directive based on the thorough assessment of the risk to trainees. Emphasis is placed on the application of a Unit Commander's Risk Assessment to determine appropriate supervisory arrangements, which depend on a range of factors, including the training activities being undertaken and the nature of each training establishment. Supervisory levels may therefore differ not only between the three Services but also between different training establishments.

Recommendation 11

Instructors must receive essential training in how they are to achieve the tasks they are to meet before they take up their post. A tour in a training regiment should be recognised as a difficult and demanding job, leading to enhanced career prospects.

The intention is for all instructors to be appropriately trained prior to taking up their posts. A competency framework for instructors is now in place, against which they will be trained and developed, and a tri-Service instructor training course ("Train the Trainer") is now being rolled out, following a successful trial. We anticipate that this course will attract civilian accreditation and should provide the first step towards the Department for Education and Skills Introductory Teaching Award Learning and Skills. We are working towards achieving, over time, mandatory attendance for all instructors prior to taking up their post, as well as ensuring that such training is also made available to instructors already in post. In the future, the Army will train all its instructors at a new staff leadership school, due to open at Pirbright in 2007, with the training conducted against standards identified and monitored by the Defence Centre of Training Support. The majority of instructors from the Royal Navy and Royal Air Force are trained at the Defence Centre of Training Support at RAF Halton.

We agree that satisfactory completion of an instructor tour should have a positive effect on an individual's subsequent career. We recognise that instructor posts have not always been recognised as career enhancing and are actively working to address this perception.

Recommendation 12

Instructors should be vetted for their suitability to work with young people, applying
standards that are no less rigorous then those applied to civilian establishments educating or
training people under 18.

We recognise the need for instructors to be checked for their suitability to work with young
people prior to taking up their posts, and we do so within the current legislative constraints.
Under the present law, Criminal Record Bureau checks do not apply to those working with under
18s in full time employment. The Ministry of Defence is therefore discussing with the Department
for Education and Skills and the Home Office changes to legislation that would allow employers
greater flexibility in carrying out Criminal Record Bureau checks on employees in the future.

In the meantime, the posting of individual Service personnel is considered by the Armed Forces
on a case-by-case basis. Every effort is made to ensure that all the relevant facts (including
career and disciplinary records) are taken into account. Improvements to this process have been
made, and we now have a much better system for identifying, flagging (on personnel files, for
example) and monitoring personnel who may have transgressed in the past. Work is underway
to review the checks that are carried out on personnel applying for instructor posts to ensure
that best practice is applied across the three Services.

Recommendation 13

A single booklet should be issued to, and signed for by, recruits and trainees when introduced
    in the induction course. The contents of such a booklet should seek to explain concisely:

(i)   what is meant by bullying and harassment;
(ii)   examples of the type of conduct that is considered inappropriate or unacceptable;
(iii) the nature and extent of acceptable sanctions that can be properly imposed and by whom;
(iv)   that blanket punishments imposed on a group for the failings of an individual are
       unacceptable; and
(v)   what a soldier should do if he or she witnesses a breach of these principles or has been a
       victim of bullying or harassment.

All recruits are already issued with information covering a wide range of issues, including: how
they should behave and how they can be expected to be treated; definitions of bullying and
harassment and what to do if such behaviour is experienced; and contact details for sources of
support and advice. In some establishments such information is issued in a single booklet. We
are now reviewing both the information and the associated process with a view to providing a
single information booklet for each Service.

In addition, the Army is currently trialling a system called "Bullytext", where trainees who may not
wish to report incidents to the chain of command can text messages to an Authorised Officer,
who will then investigate the matter. Early indications are that this is seen as a useful additional
support mechanism.

Recommendation 14

Cancellation of weekend leave by an NCO is not a permissible informal punishment. This should be explained in the booklet issued to trainees.

Leave should not be cancelled without good reason and the authority of the Officer Commanding. Good reason for cancellation should be explained to the trainee at the time.

The allocation of guard duty should never be used as a punishment.

Loss of leave cannot be awarded as a punishment, but not being able to go on leave may be a consequence of other punishments, or of course because of Service reasons. Where time off has to be cancelled for any reason, it must be explained to the individual. A new corrective training policy is currently being trialled at a range of training establishments. It includes the requirement that if corrective training is to be carried out at weekends, it is to be authorised only by a Commissioned Officer, on behalf of the Commanding Officer.

Additional guard duty is currently a permissible administrative sanction for the Army. However, we will ensure that implementation of this sanction is limited to failings whilst on guard duty, as a means of correcting professional failings. The Armed Forces Bill will remove the current provision for additional guarding duty to be awarded at a summary trial.

Recommendation 15

The standards set by the ATRA Code of Practice for Instructors should be enforced by formal disciplinary sanctions. Training regiments should adopt standing orders that require adherence to the Code of Practice to enable charges under the Army Act, or for breach of standing orders, to be brought. Breach of such standards should also be admissible evidence in a charge of "ill treatment" of subordinates.

The Defence Centre of Training Support published a Defence Instructors' Handbook in 2005, which includes a Code of Practice for instructors. This is being reviewed and is due to be re-published in the coming months. In most cases, failure to adhere to the code would be viewed as a professional failing best dealt with through administrative action. In some cases, a breach of the code may amount to a disciplinary matter in itself, or may be used in evidence to support a charge.

Recommendation 16

Every Officer, NCO, civilian instructor and trainee should be alert to both expressions of intention to self-harm, however trivial or jocular they may seem at the time, and to any breaches of standing orders designed to promote safety. Such matters must be reported through the chain of command, so prompt and effective action can be taken.

As the Review recognises, the risk of future self-inflicted deaths cannot be wholly eradicated. However, we are fully committed to ensuring that everyone is aware of the signs of the intention to self-harm, and how concerns should be reported through the chain of command, in order to reduce that risk as far as possible. Training is being implemented, at all levels, on the identification and management of both operational and workplace stress, and guidance (such as information leaflets) and procedures on the prevention and management of suicide and self-harm continue to be updated. Each of the Services has specific policies on suicide risk management. In the Army's case a policy on Suicide Vulnerability Risk Management provides detailed and mandatory guidance about how to identify those at risk of suicide and how to manage and care for them. Furthermore, additional suicide awareness training has recently been introduced into the mandatory Unit Welfare Officers course at Bristol University, which all Army Unit Welfare Officers attend.

All three Services have established confidential support lines that provide a fully trained, confidential, independent and non-judgemental listening and support service. Further work is in progress covering prevention, screening, reporting, data collection, training and education.

Our practices are kept under review to ensure that best practice is implemented across all three Services.

Recommendation 17

Every Officer, NCO, civilian instructor and trainee should be alert to any sign of abuse and be required to report it through the chain of command, so prompt and effective action can be taken.

We expect our personnel to behave to the highest of standards. At every stage of a Service person's career it is made very clear that the Armed Forces do not tolerate any form of bullying and harassment, and this is enshrined in the Armed Forces' Code of Social Conduct. All Service personnel are informed of the means by which they can bring any allegations of such conduct to the attention of the correct authority. We encourage any allegation of inappropriate behaviour to be raised to the attention of the Commanding Officer so it can be investigated and dealt with accordingly, and Service personnel have a duty to report any such offences.

Recommendation 18

Failure to report any sign of abuse of power should itself be a matter for disciplinary sanction.

We believe that Service personnel at all levels are well aware of their responsibility to report any allegation of inappropriate behaviour. Where this amounts to a culpable failure, the normal disciplinary or administrative procedures would be applied.

Recommendation 19

There should be an instruction that:

(i)   policy documents be regularly reviewed in the light of experience;
(ii) previous versions of policies and instructions be kept centrally with a record of when and why changes were made; and
(iii) clear policies be established for the destruction or retention of classes of documents, the authority needed for destruction and the records needed to be kept of the fact of such destruction.

We accept that the identification and recovery of past documents has been less than ideal. Improvements have been made to address this through new methods of storing and handling documents electronically. In addition, a Defence Records Management Manual has been issued as a Joint Service Publication. Policies are constantly kept under review and amendments and updates are made as appropriate. An internal programme of visits to training establishments includes an analysis of the purpose, interpretation and implementation of departmental training policies, with a view to ensuring that they achieve the desired effect.

Further improvements will continue to be made as we tackle this sizeable task and work towards achieving this recommendation over time.

Recommendation 20

The Army should convene a multi-disciplinary case conference of all the interested military agencies to examine the available papers relating to the case of Sergeant BB, with a view to developing a common approach to the detection and deterrence of abuse.

The case conference was convened. An initial assessment of the findings reveals that a number of the systemic failings at the time should not be possible now, as a result of a series of measures designed to prevent unsuitable individuals being assigned to training posts and to allow complaints to be aired. The detailed consideration of the case identified a number of other more minor issues that need to be addressed to further improve the checking procedures.

Recommendation 21

All reasonable steps should be taken to encourage early reporting of complaints against staff by ensuring:

(i)   there is a prompt and thorough investigation, independent of the unit whose members are the subject of complaint;
(ii) all suitable interim measures are taken to protect the complainant from retribution, including removal from the unit of the alleged perpetrator of the conduct complained;
(iii) information is supplied to the complainant on the outcome of the investigation; and
(iv) appropriate disciplinary and/or administrative action is taken.

AND

Recommendation 22

Complaints of mistreatment, bullying and harassment should be promptly assigned to the RMP to investigate and report on, so that appropriate disciplinary and/or administrative action can be taken.

The Ministry of Defence strongly encourages any allegation of inappropriate behaviour to be reported promptly and requires them to be investigated accordingly. Many cases can be dealt with quickly and effectively by the chain of command, in a way that is satisfactory to the complainant. In other cases, such as those that are more serious and those where the chain of command is itself the subject of the complaint, external investigation by the Service Police or by Equal Opportunities Investigation Teams would be adopted.

It is current practice that during an investigation measures should be taken to protect the complainant if necessary, which may involve the removal of either the complainant or alleged perpetrator from the unit. We agree that complainants should be kept fully informed of the progress of their complaint, and that administrative or disciplinary action should be taken in cases where this is justified. A review of the Ministry of Defence Harassment Complaints Procedures is underway and it is intended that updated guidance will be published around the end of the year.

Recommendation 23

RMP training should be kept under review to ensure that investigators are skilled in best practice in interviewing complainants, recording their accounts, pursuing lines of enquiry in investigations and that they are aware of the particular problems that may arise where the alleged perpetrator retaliates, or others turn, against a complainant.

We are committed to the professionalism of the Service Police and maintain a continuous review of training and standards. As a result, improvements have already taken place. The formation of the Defence Police College in late 2005 standardised Service police training. Training in relation to offences which, due to their seriousness or complexity require investigation by Special Investigation Branch personnel, and which includes specialist interviewing techniques and dealing with vulnerable witnesses, mirrors the training undertaken by Home Office Police Forces and follows Association of Chief Police Officers guidelines.

Continuous review will continue, in line with the practices of Home Office Police Forces and Association of Chief Police Officers guidelines.

Recommendation 24

The RMP should be brought within the regime of inspection of Her Majesty's Inspectorate of Constabulary (HMIC) so that the consistent application of best practice in the investigation of crimes and complaints can be monitored. HMIC can determine whether the RMP is sufficiently well-resourced and appropriately trained to perform the functions assigned to it.

Agreement has been reached with Her Majesty's Inspectorate of Constabulary (HMIC) for a thematic inspection of the Royal Military Police's (RMP) Special Investigations Branch, which is now underway. A report is anticipated in the summer, after which we will assess with Her Majesty's Inspectorate of Constabulary how inspection may be carried out more widely across the Services' police forces.

We propose to develop further these inspection arrangements, as discussed later in the response to Recommendation 26.

Recommendation 25

There should be a minimum standard for the recording of information in respect of complaints. Such records should specifically explain what disciplinary and/or administrative action was taken, with justification, and note the outcome. A decision not to take any action should also be recorded in the same way. Documentation should be retained for at least six years.

We have already sought to improve the recording and retention of information in respect of the management of complaints. A Defence Instruction and Notice (DIN) was released in December 2005 on the maintenance of Unit Equality and Diversity logs, which are used to record and report all incidents and complaints of bullying and harassment. We are now looking at how further improvements may be made with regard to the wider complaints process.

Recommendation 26

There should be established a Commissioner of Military Complaints (the Armed Forces Ombudsman) who should be a person independent of the three Services with at least the functions set out in paragraph 12.101 [of the Deepcut Review].

The Deepcut Review states that this recommendation is designed to promote the effective operation of existing military proceedings, rather than to replace them, and to provide independent assurance that the procedures are working as effectively as they can. Similarly, the Government's overall objective is to have a complaints system that is right for the way our Armed Forces operate: that is fair, transparent, effective and prompt, and in which both the chain of command and the individual Service person can have confidence.

Some of the detailed functions identified in the Review for a commissioner would be difficult to reconcile with these core principles. The ability to intervene in the handling of a complaint, or to supervise the investigations of or response to a complaint, are not appropriate for an independent commissioner and would risk undermining the chain of command and its overall responsibilities for the welfare of those under command. The proposal that a commissioner might have the right to be consulted in disciplinary matters, or have the ability to intervene to institute legal proceedings against decisions not to prosecute, would undermine the role and independence of the prosecuting authorities. There is no precedent in the civilian criminal justice system for such intervention. The independent prosecuting authorities make their decisions on the basis of evidential tests and public or Service interest tests, under the general superintendence of the Attorney General.

The Government believes, however, that the key purposes underlying the Review's recommendations could be met by the provisions already proposed under the Armed Forces Bill, with some adjustment. The Bill already provides for an independent element in the complaints process. Where a Service complaint panel deals with complaints relating to bullying and harassment, it will contain an independent member, who would be able to share fully in the exercise of the panel's powers on behalf of the Defence Council. There would, in addition, be an independent external reviewer who would examine the fairness and effectiveness of the military complaints system and report annually to Ministers. The report would be published.

In the light of the Review's recommendation, and taking account of evidence given to the Select Committee on the Bill, we propose to go further. We propose to give the external reviewer a wider role, in relation to complaints of bullying and harassment. He would be able to receive complaints directly from Service personnel, or allegations made on their behalf by family members or other third parties, and have the power to refer them to the chain of command for action. He would also be entitled to be notified of the outcome. This should not undermine the responsibility of the chain of command and it would provide another avenue for a matter to be raised by any who might be reluctant to approach the Commanding Officer directly. We would reflect this wider role for the external reviewer by changing the title to 'Service Complaints Commissioner'. The Commissioner would have direct access to Ministers.

Further, we propose to develop our existing use of independent inspection arrangements by the Chief Inspector of Prisons, Her Majesty's Inspector of Constabulary and the Adult Learning Inspectorate. The Government will be creating a new combined inspectorate for the criminal justice system, under the Police and Justice Bill, and we intend to use the opportunity to extend and deepen inspection arrangements across the military justice system. Those working in the military justice system would welcome such external assurance to demonstrate their professionalism and ability to work to standards comparable to those of the criminal justice system, while respecting the unique characteristics of military life.

These proposed arrangements will now be subject to the full process of Parliamentary scrutiny, and the passage of the Armed Forces Bill offers an early opportunity for such examination and debate.

Taken together, we believe that the proposed arrangements will meet the aims behind the Review's recommendation, though in some practical respects they are, for good reason, different from those suggested by the Review.

Recommendation 27

(i)   The performance of armed guard duty by a trainee of any age should be directly supervised by an NCO, experienced adult soldier or MPGS guard.

(ii) To ensure that there is no unsupervised access to weapons, trainees under 18 should only perform guard duty (whether armed or unarmed) as part of training and when directly supervised by an NCO, experienced adult soldier or MPGS guard.

(iii) The minimum age for trained soldiers in the field army to conduct unsupervised armed guard duty should be 18.

Armed guarding, across all three Services, is restricted by reference to age, qualification in weapons handling, supervision and stage of training, though there are some differences between the Services reflecting different circumstances and requirements. No Phase 1 trainees may undertake armed guarding.

Current Army policy is that Phase 2 trainees over 17 who have passed the appropriate weapon handling tests may undertake armed patrols if accompanied by another appropriately trained soldier. Any detachment isolated from the main guard is to be commanded by a Non-Commissioned Officer (NCO). In the Royal Navy and Royal Marines, armed guarding may be undertaken only by those under 18s who have completed Phase 1 and Phase 2 training and have qualified in weapons handling. No armed guarding is currently carried out by Royal Air Force trainees under 18; after the completion of Phase 1 and Phase 2 training, suitably qualified Royal Air Force personnel over the age of 17 may undertake armed guarding under the supervision of a Non-Commissioned Officer.

Under current policy, no under 18s may undertake armed guarding alone, even if they are fully trained and qualified in weapons handling; they must always be accompanied.

In the longer term, it is expected that the recruitment of additional numbers to the Military Provost Guard Service will obviate the need for Phase 2 trainees to undertake routine guard duty.

Recommendation 28

There should be full and prompt disclosure of information to the nominated next of kin of the fact of, and the circumstances then known about, the death of any soldier. Trainees should be encouraged to nominate both parents as their next of kin.

Policy is already in place covering the prompt and full disclosure of information to nominated next of kin of the fact of, and the circumstances then known about, the death of any Service person. As much information as possible is provided to next of kin in the early stages, although there may be some necessary restrictions if there is any possibility of criminal charges being brought. Where this is the case, Police Family Liaison Officers (either military or civilian) will explain why some information cannot be released at that time and keep the next of kin informed of progress.

The introduction of the Joint Personnel Administration system, currently being rolled out, will enable Service personnel to record as many family members as they like as next of kin, but in practice the nomination of two will be the norm.

Recommendation 29

After the death of a soldier, there should be appointed a military liaison officer, as well as a civilian police liaison officer. The military liaison officer should be the single point of contact to explain procedures for the funeral, the return of property of the deceased soldier and, where the RMP have primacy, the progress of the investigations.

Whilst we accept that there have been shortcomings in the past, current practice fulfils this recommendation. A military Visiting Officer is always appointed whether there is a civilian or military Family Liaison Officer appointed by the police or Special Investigations Branch. Close liaison takes place to ensure that there is no duplication. The Visiting Officer explains all investigatory procedures, funeral arrangements and disposal of effects, as well as progress in the investigation if there are no potential criminal charges.

For the Army, this process is overseen by the Army Inquiries and Aftercare Support Cell, which was formed in May 2005 expressly to ensure proper liaison with bereaved families. Analogous arrangements exist for the other two Services.

Recommendation 30

There should always be an inquest, or, in Scotland, a Fatal Accidents Inquiry, into a sudden death of a soldier, wherever the death has occurred.

Discussions are continuing between the Ministry of Defence and the Department for Constitutional Affairs with a view to responding to this recommendation in the draft Coroners Bill. Responsibility for legislation on inquiries into deaths in Scotland is devolved to the Scottish administration and the recommendation will therefore be discussed with the Scottish Executive.

Recommendation 31

As part of the Military Covenant with the soldier, the MOD should ensure that the family of a deceased soldier have access to legal advice and, where appropriate, legal representation prior to, and during, the inquest or FAI.

An inquest is an inquisitorial, non-adversarial fact finding process of limited scope which does not make findings of civil or criminal liability. It is the general presumption that legal representation is not necessary, and it is quite appropriate for those deemed interested persons by the Coroner to ask questions of witnesses at an inquest without legal assistance. Government provision of legal aid through the Legal Services Commission is not therefore normally available to interested persons. However, under the Access to Justice Act 1998 application may be made to the Legal Services Commission for exceptional funding.

Recommendation 32

Where there is a Board of Inquiry (BOI):

(i) The family of a deceased or injured soldier should be permitted to attend and be offered the opportunity to add information that may be relevant and otherwise participate as circumstances require.
(ii) The family should receive all statements and reports into the death that they indicate they would like to see, and should see a copy of the BOI's final report.
(iii) Such participation and disclosure of information should only be restricted by particularly compelling public interest considerations. The privacy concerns of witnesses to such a procedure would not generally suffice to justify restriction of access and disclosure.

We accept that where family members have relevant information they should be invited to provide it to the Board of Inquiry, as witnesses, and that as much information from the Board of Inquiry should be released to them as possible. We do not believe, however, that the interests of the Board of Inquiry, or of the families themselves, would be best served by changing the nature of the Board of Inquiry to make it a public hearing at which family members (or others) have a right to be present.

A Board of Inquiry is an internal Service investigation, the sole purpose of which is to establish the facts of a particular incident and make recommendations in order to prevent it happening again. It does not replace a Coroner's Inquest and is not, and does not purport to be, a tribunal that is compliant with Article 2 of the European Convention on Human Rights. Boards of Inquiry are not open to the public, press or family members unless they are called as a witness. The principle reason for this is that a public hearing, or a hearing at which family members have a right to be present, could serve to inhibit the provision of full and frank evidence from witnesses and so detract generally from the prime purpose of the Board of Inquiry. There is also a practical consideration, in that a Board of Inquiry could convene and adjourn several times over a number of months, potentially in different locations around the world and often in operational theatres.

Significant improvements have already been made to procedures to ensure that families are more closely involved in the inquiry and investigation into the circumstances surrounding the death of their loved one. Families are invited to submit questions that they would like answered to the Board of Inquiry, they may provide evidence to the Board of Inquiry in person if this is appropriate and they are kept fully informed of progress. They are provided with a copy of the Board of Inquiry's final report (which may be redacted only due to necessary third party data and security considerations) and they are offered personal briefings at the conclusion of the Board of Inquiry.

Finally, we accept that there may be circumstances in which a family attendance at a particular Board of Inquiry would be acceptable, where it would not impede the Board of Inquiry. In these circumstances, discretion may be exercised.

Recommendation 33

The Review recommends to Surrey Police that the families of Sean Benton, Cheryl James and Geoff Gray be provided with copies of the respective Surrey Police report, and supporting witness statements, into their child's death, solely for the purpose of considering whether an application should be made to the High Court to set aside the previous inquest in their child's death. Such disclosure may need to be subject to an agreement or undertaking by the families, and their legal advisers, as to disclosure to third parties and/or subject to editing of any highly confidential information to which public interest immunity may apply.

This recommendation is a matter for the Surrey Police. It is therefore for them to consider and act on as they see appropriate. However, we believe that the Review has helpfully drawn attention to the process by which an inquest may be re-opened. The Ministry of Defence would of course co-operate fully in such an eventuality.

Recommendation 34

In the opinion of this Review, for the reasons set out above, a Public Inquiry into the immediate or broader circumstances surrounding these deaths is not necessary.

We share this view and, given the extensive investigations that have taken place, see no public or Service interest in pursuing a Public Inquiry. We now need to ensure that lessons are learned from these tragic events, that improvements continue to be made so that we provide the best possible care for all our personnel, and that we do everything we can to ensure that such incidents do not happen again.

Printed in the UK by The Stationery Office Limited
on behalf of the Controller of Her Majesty's Stationery Office
ID 188264 06/06